LET'S EXPLORE THE LONE STAR STATE, Y'ALL!

Welcome to Texas

DRIVE FRIENDLY - THE TEXAS WAY

TEXAS Wildflowers

BLUEBONNET

INDIAN BLANKET

INDIAN PAINTBRUSH

BLACK EYED SUSAN

PINK EVENING PRIMROSE

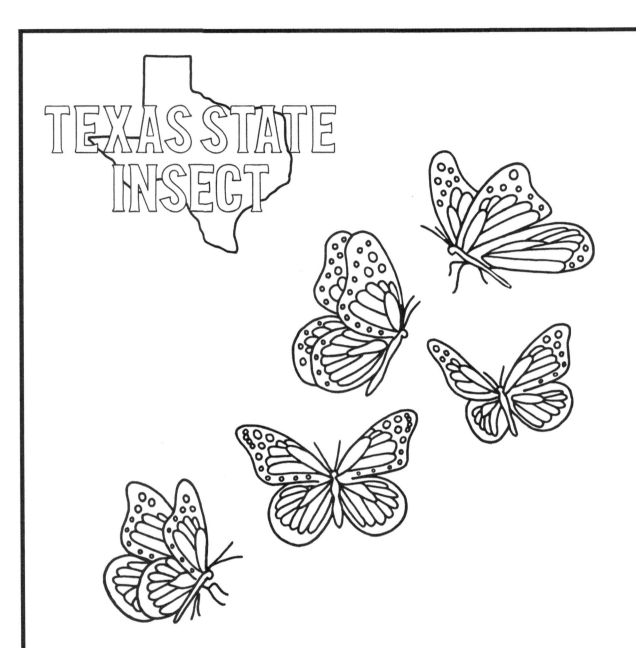

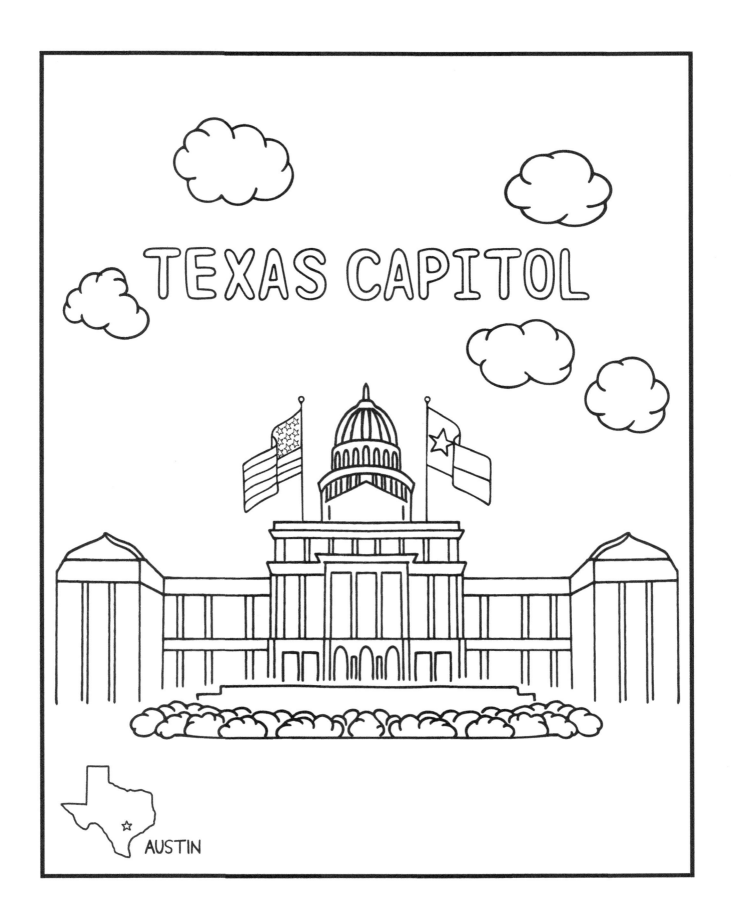

☆ TEXAS FLAGS ☆

DE ZAVALA
FIRST REPUBLIC FLAG

BATTLE OF GONZALES
FLAG

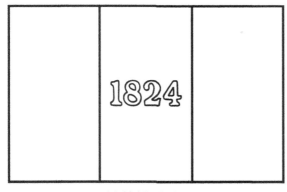

ALAMO FLAG

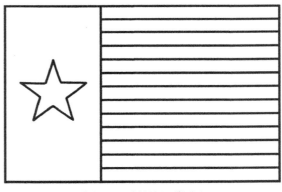

FIRST NAVAL FLAG
OF TEXAS

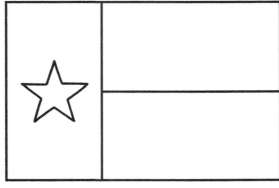

TEXAS STATE FLAG

ANIMALS OF TEXAS

WHITE TAILED DEER

ARMADILLO

LONGHORN

MEXICAN FREE TAILED BAT

BLACK TAILED JACK RABBIT

MOCKINGBIRD

TEXAS HORNED LIZARD

ROADRUNNER

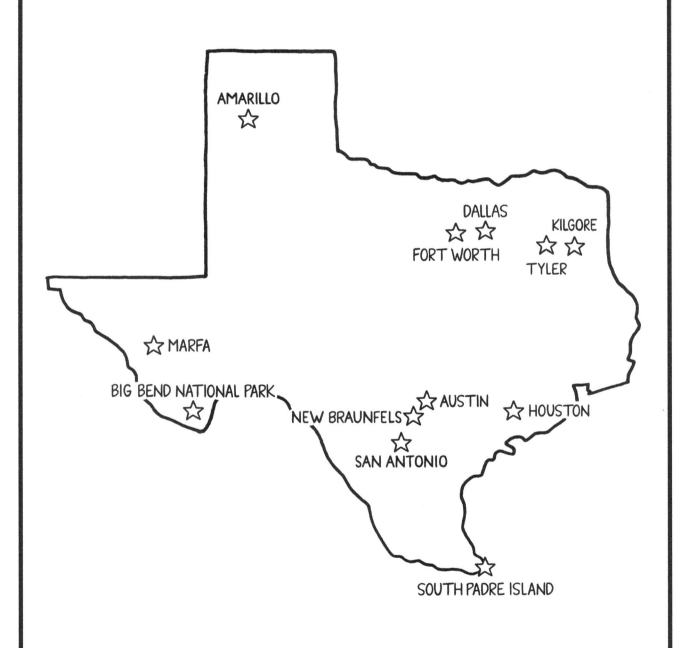